SOCIAL ANXIETY

An introvert's step by step guide to overcome social anxiety, shyness and low confidence - accept yourself without giving up who you are

Wallace Foulds

Text Copyright © 2018 Wallace Foulds

Legal & Disclaimer

The information contained in this book is not designed to replace or take the place of any form of medicine or professional medical advice. The information in this book has been provided for educational and entertainment purposes only.

The information contained in this book has been compiled from sources deemed reliable, and it is accurate to the best of the Author's knowledge; however, the Author cannot guarantee its accuracy and validity and cannot be held liable for any errors or omissions. Changes are periodically made to this book. You must consult your doctor or get professional medical advice before using any of the suggested remedies, techniques, or information in this book.

Upon using the information contained in this book, you agree to hold harmless the Author from and against any damages, costs, and expenses, including any legal fees potentially resulting from the application of any of the information provided by this guide. This disclaimer applies to any damages or injury caused by the use and application, whether directly or indirectly, of any advice or information presented, whether for breach of contract, tort, negligence, personal injury, criminal intent, or under any other cause of action.

You agree to accept all risks of using the information presented inside this book. You need to consult a professional medical practitioner in order to ensure you are both able and healthy enough to participate in this program.

TABLE OF CONTENTS

INTRODUCTION

Every one of us feels anxious at some points in our lives, which is quite normal. Getting anxious is a natural human reaction and that is not inherently problematic. Quite the contrary— anxiety serves an important biological function. We experience this emotion in many different ways— physically, emotionally, and in the way we view the world around us. But when our fear response does not work properly, we may experience extreme irrational fear about a situation, activity or object. When you have something— or many things that cause you excessive, unreasonable fear, then you have developed a phobia. A phobia sufferer can go to extreme lengths to avoid an object or situation that can scare them. They often realize their fear is irrational and that no real danger is present, but despite their best effort, they fail to overcome their overwhelming, persistent anxiety. Even the thought of their object of fear, makes them scared.

It is believed that everyone suffers from one phobia or another, to varying degrees. Impact of a phobia can be different for different individuals— it can range from irritating to extremely disabling. If you notice that your avoidance of the object of fear is interfering with your normal routine or causing significant distress and holding you back from doing things, it may time to seek help.

Scientists have identified more than 400 distinct phobias. Some are more common than others. This book is devoted to helping the readers to overcome one of the most common phobias that plagues millions of people: "Social Phobia" or "Social Anxiety Disorder (SAD)".

People with social anxiety feel scared to participate in the simplest social encounters. They experience extreme persistent fear of being watched, scrutinized or judged by others, which leads to feeling of inferiority, inadequacy and embarrassment. For some people, social anxiety can be limited to one type of situation, but for others the symptoms can be surfaced anytime they are around other people.

Many of us encounter lesser form of social anxiety in situations like public speaking event, mingling with clients or first date, which we identify as shyness or occasional nerves. But social anxiety disorder is more than just "normal shyness". It's an overwhelming fear that causes us to struggle to deal with social encounters in a healthy manner, which affects our everyday activities, self-confidence, relationships and work life.

Overcoming social anxiety may not be an easy task, but it is very much possible. This book is designed as a step-by-step guide to overcome social anxiety and shyness using the most powerful self-help strategies. No matter how severe you think your condition is, you can eliminate or significantly limit your social anxiety by applying the methods included in this book.

It is recommended to read the chapters in order, because each chapter builds upon what is covered in the previous chapter.

CHAPTER 1

UNDERSTANDING SOCIAL ANXIETY

American Psychiatric Association in the *Diagnostic and Statistical Manual of Mental Disorders* (4th edition; 1994; p 416) defined social anxiety disorder as, " A marked and persistent fear of one or more social or performance situations in which the person is exposed to unfamiliar people or possible scrutiny by others. The person fears that he or she will act in a way that will be humiliating or embarrassing"

This means that social anxiety is about your perceived fear of what others might think about you. The social encounters feared by individuals may vary widely, but most common ones are public speaking, talking to strangers, asking someone for a first date, and being assertive. Other situations may include being a center of attention, eating or drinking in front of others, talking with an authority figure, urinating in a public toilet (avoidant paruresis or shy bladder syndrome— males with social anxiety usually experience this symptom) or intimate sexual situations. Regardless of the feared situations, social anxiety sufferers share a common fear that others will think negatively of them. Sometimes their fear of what others think makes them experience anxiety symptoms like blushing and trembling.

An individual must meet the following criteria to be diagnosed with social phobia or social anxiety disorder.

- The individual must realize that the social situations that make them extremely anxious are not much frightening for most people.

- The individual must avoid their feared social situations or go through extreme distress if they must face them.

- Their condition must significantly interfere with their lives (e.g. making them staying at home, keeping them from dating, going to work, meeting friends)

Most people experience social anxiety sometimes, and it disappears as soon as the threat is gone. It does not interfere with the person's life. But social anxiety disorder is a severe form of anxiety, which is experienced in most social encounters. If you don't technically meet the above criteria and not sure whether this program is appropriate for you, answer the following questions.

1. Do you feel shy and nervous around people, and your nervousness stops you from doing things you need to do?

2. Have you avoided looking for a better job only because you are scared of interacting with unfamiliar people? If you are unemployed, does the fear of dealing with unknown persons, and job interviews keep you from seeking employment?

3. Do you usually avoid the invitations for social events because you know social gatherings make you feel terrible?

4. Does your fear of possible embarrassment make you avoid dating?

5. Does your perception of fear in interaction stops you from getting involved with others? Do you believe that if people really knew the real you, they would dislike you?

6. Do you feel relieved if your planned social event or group activity is cancelled?

7. Are you worried about blushing or looking nervous in social encounters?

8. Do you rarely start a small talk with neighbors, shopkeepers and passengers traveling next to you on the train, bus or plane?

9. Do you feel anxious entering a room where everyone already seated?

10. Does being a center of attention make you feel awkward?

11. Do you feel uncomfortable eating in front of others?

12. Do you daydream a lot about being a social person or being a center of attention?

If your answer to most of the questions is "yes", then this book is for you.

Mental health professionals distinguish two kinds of social phobia for diagnostic purposes: non-generalized and generalized social phobia. For the individuals with non-generalized social phobia, the anxiety symptoms are relatively limited and confined in few performance situations such as being with opposite sex, addressing a group of people or writing in public. This can be a serious problem for some people, but most people with non-generalized social phobia function well in other types of social situations.

Individuals with generalized social phobia are likely to experience anxiety in most situations involving interaction with others. They often feel self-conscious and uncomfortable in kinds of social situations that most people take for granted— talking to strangers, eating in front of others and attending social events. Sufferers of generalized social phobia may find the situations they fear are so all pervasive that there are relatively few areas where they function comfortably.

We've also used the term "shyness" in this book. There are similarities between shyness and social anxiety. People who are shy but not diagnosed with social anxiety disorder may find some of the social anxiety symptoms match their conditions. That does not mean that they are having a psychological disorder, but reflects the fact that social anxiety and shyness appear in varying degrees and that its impact can be more or less troublesome.

ELEMENTS OF SOCIAL ANXIETY

The physiological component: The physiological aspect of social anxiety explains the physical symptoms you experience during social encounters. You may experience the similar symptoms for other conditions. For example, an anxious person can feel nauseous, but you can also feel nauseous if you feel sick to your stomach, especially after you eat rich fatty meal. These symptoms also indicate a medical condition in rare occasions. For example rapid heartbeat and tightness in the chest experienced during anxiety may also suggest heart problems. However if you find that these symptoms only appear when you are stressed or worried about something, then these are most likely the signs of anxiety disorder. Common symptoms include:

- Blushing

- Rapid heartbeat

- Profuse sweating

- Trembling

- Dizziness or light headedness

- Palpitations

- Blurred vision

- Upset stomach or nausea

- Muscle tension

- Shortness of breath

- Pain in the chest

- Tightness in the chest

- Lump in the throat

- Shaky voice

- Cold and clammy hands

- Paresthesia (tingling sensation in the toes, fingers and face)

- Headache

- Depersonalization (feeling as if your surroundings are not the way they should be)

One in every three social anxiety sufferer has experienced a very particular combination of symptoms at least once in their lifetime. This anxiety symptom is called "panic attack". During panic attack, the sufferer goes through a quick rush of anxiety, which is comprised of at least four of the following symptoms:

1. Profuse sweating

2. Racing or pounding heart

3. Dizziness, faintness or unsteady feelings

4. Shortness of breath

5. Shaking or trembling

6. Hot flashes or chills

7. Depersonalization

8. Nausea or abdominal discomfort

9. Tightness of chest or chest pain

10. Numbness

11. Choking

12. Fear of losing control or fear of going crazy

13. Fear of death

While having a panic attack, an individual experiences any four of the above symptoms simultaneously. This is the moment where the anxiety reaches the highest peak. The duration of panic attack is usually depends on the individual and what triggers it. Most panic attacks takes around 10 minutes from start to finish. But because of the intensity of physical symptoms, you may feel that you're stuck in this frightening state for a long time. You may have noticed that the last two symptoms of panic attack are not physical symptoms. People, who experience a panic attack for the first time, think that they are about to lose their mind or have a heart attack. This happens because in this stage the anxiety peaks at its highest level and it feels overwhelming. For most people, a panic attack is a one-time occurrence, but for some people, it is a regular experience. People who have panic attacks spontaneously and at times when they don't expect it, their condition can be termed as "panic disorder". While experiencing a panic attack a social phobic is usually more worried about whether other people noticing their condition than the physical symptoms themselves. On the other hand, individuals with other anxiety disorders are more concerned about the physical symptoms.

Almost a fourth of the people who visit emergency rooms because of chest pain are actually experiencing panic attack. But panic attack is never a life-threatening emergency. Therefore if you ever experience a panic attack, keep in mind that it is a harmless feeling.

The cognitive component: The cognitive component of social anxiety is concerned with the mental process such as perception and thinking. When we experience anxiety in social situations its quite common to have thoughts running through our mind. Depending on the individuals and the situation they are in, the content of the thought may vary. But the common theme may include:

- They think I'm weird

- They don't like me

- What if ......happens?

- I'm going crazy

- People will laugh at me

- The person X looked distant today, I must've offended him/her

- I won't be able to escape

- I don't deserve this

- I'm an idiot

- I'm never good enough

- There is no hope for me

As everyone is unique, the possible worrisome thoughts may vary depending on the individual's own unique anxiety history and the nature of their anxiety.

The behavioral component: In psychology, behavior refers to an organism's external reactions to its environment. When psychologists talk about behavior, they usually mean anything that we can observe others are doing. Behavioral components are what the anxiety sufferers do (or don't do) when they are anxious. A sufferer of social phobia may exhibit the following behavioral responses while attempting to cope with the unpleasant aspects of anxiety.

- Avoidance behavior: avoiding anxiety producing situations (e.g. social events) or places (e.g. using stairs instead of an elevator)

- Escape behavior: escaping from situations that produce anxiety (e.g. a crowded meeting room)

- Safety behavior such as siting in the back of the room to avoid excessive scrutiny or wearing neutral clothing to avoid drawing attention to oneself and in severe cases, refusing to go out, away from home.

- Gaze aversion: averting eye contact to avoid being noticed by others.

- Substance abuse: engaging in unhealthy and self-destructive behaviors such as drinking excessively or taking drugs.

- Reducing the amount of daily activities to decrease the level of anxiety (e.g. staying in the safety of one's home)

Avoidance behavior is an interesting aspect of social anxiety, because avoiding feared situations provides a short-term relief. But in the long run it generates bigger problems. A person who starts to avert particular social encounters to avoid anxiety unknowingly develops a general pattern of avoiding lots of situations. It gradually becomes harder for them to quit avoiding anxiety provoking situations because of the immediate relief avoidance provides. This immediate relief is the "reward" of avoidance, which motivates the individual to avoid more situations.

Social anxiety sufferers tend to escape notice and stay out of spotlight at any cost. They fear being singled out for criticism; even praise in front of a group is experienced as suffering, with so many people witnessing their discomfort (e.g. blushing) and ensuing disgrace.

They try to stay out of trouble and lead a blameless life. Social phobic individuals are usually perfectionists. They try their best to eliminate the possibility of mistakes or being in the wrong.

They are not very eager to take charges and allow others to take important decisions. They tend to give in to pressure or intimidation or at least give that impression. If they fail to comply, they resort to elaborate justification in a fear of offending others. When embarrassed (e.g. being criticized or praised) they avert gaze, giggle nervously or blush. According to Stein & Bouwer (1997), this disarming pattern can be considered an appeasement or a submission display in a bid to mitigate threats from their potentially hostile counterparts.

People with social anxiety seek a sense of security in other's approval. They try hard to present themselves agreeable— they smile, nod with interest and approval with those they know. They try to carefully conceal their disappointment or resentment because of fear of retaliation. Maintaining a relationship sometimes becomes a struggle for them.

WHAT CAUSES SOCIAL ANXIETY?

Like many other psychological disorders, the causes of social anxiety are multifactorial. That means it is not caused by one thing, but results from a combination of factors including prior experiences, negative thinking, genetic predisposition and for some a paucity of social skills.

Genetic Predisposition: There is not such gene that is directly responsible for social anxiety. However in the last twenty years lots of research has been done, and some studies indicate that for some social phobic individuals, the condition may have a genetic link. While studying social anxiety among twins, the researchers found that if one twin is social phobic the other twin is likely to be social phobic. This likelihood is higher among the identical twins (developed from a single fertilized egg that split into two) than the fraternal twins.

Jerome Kargan a Harvard researcher and his team found another evidence that suggests the role of genetics in the development of social anxiety disorder. Dr. Kargan identified a behavioral trait among some infants what he termed as, "behavioral inhibition to the unfamiliar". Those infants were only few months old and were followed to the age of seven. Kargan found that three in every four children who were uncomfortable with the unfamiliar continued to be shy and three of every four children who were not uncomfortable were not shy at the age 7. As the shyness or discomfort was present from childhood and seemed to last as the child developed, it may support the theory that for some people, social phobia can be traced to a genetic link.

Many social phobic individuals think that they have inherited their condition from their parents. If you are severely social phobic, there are probably other members of your family who are socially anxious or at least a bit shy. A person with social anxiety is about three times as likely to have a close family member with the same condition as a person who is not social phobic. Although it is clear that social phobia runs in families, researchers are not sure if it is a learned behavior or whether there is any biological basis. Now, even if a person's social anxiety is caused by an inherited component or "bad gene", it is also treatable and curable; because genetic contribution to all psychological disorders including social anxiety is a predisposition, not a blueprint. If you have a genetic predisposition of shyness, there is an increased likelihood that you will be shy; but whether or not you'll develop social anxiety depends on many other factors including your life's experience.

Environmental factor: The family environment can contribute greatly in the development in one's anxiety. The family affects our personality, behavior and the way we see the world. Much of what we know about ourselves and how the world works, we learned from our family when we grew up. Our core beliefs about life start to form from early childhood, which are the strongest factors that influence our personality. These beliefs may include who and what we are, whether or not we can trust others, how much control do we have over our lives and whether other people and circumstances control our lives. We also start to know whether we are valuable or whether we deserve respect. We watch and listen to the people around us and learn all those basic principles.

Children can learn to be socially anxious from parents if one or both parents are socially anxious. For instance, if the parents have social anxiety disorder, they tend not to socialize with other families, and their children will learn to avoid socialization. If a parent feels nervous and uncomfortable around people and always worried about what other's think, he or she may unwittingly teach their child that social situations are not safe and should be avoided. When a child is worried about a social encounter, socially anxious parents suggest them to avoid it. As a result, the child starts to avoid more social situations, which eventually leads to generalized social phobia.

Other kinds of family environment may also contribute to social anxiety. If a child grows up in a family environment where the following conditions are typical, they can also develop social anxiety symptoms:

- There are lots of conflicts between the parents

- Parents are overly critical of their children. They seek perfection and blame themselves or their children when things are not right.

Many children are shy or mildly social anxious and they overcome their condition on their own. Even some severely anxious young children grow out of their anxiety without any special help. Children, who overcome their anxiety problem on their own, learn through repeated experiences that social anxiety is not real; there is very little need to be afraid to talk in front of a group or taking small challenges.

However there is no way to know whether your children will outgrow their shyness. If you are a parent and find your child has been unusually shy since age six and now at age ten no improvement is visible, there is a good chance the problem will persist. If they display other symptoms such as depression and low self-esteem, don't wait to see if they will outgrow it—take necessary steps. Motivate your children to take challenges, add fun activities to your family routine, and encourage them to participate in hobbies and other social and leisure pursuits.

Life's experiences: People may develop anxiety from experiences. This type of social anxiety is formed in childhood or adolescence and continues throughout life. A child who is teased or bullied because of being different may grow up as a social phobic. For instance, if a child is teased for stuttering may gradually develop avoidance behavior that leads to social anxiety. Speech difficulty may disappear in time or thorough speech therapy treatment, but their anxiety may persist.

Some social anxiety sufferers reported that their problem began after having a panic attack in a social situation. For instance, some individuals with glossophobia (public speaking anxiety) remember having an experience of panic attack in a public speaking event and which made them feeling embarrassed and humiliated. Some of them had to quit their speech because of too much anxiety. Although, these occurrences are not uncommon is schools, some people can't forget the feeling of embarrassment. Their traumatic memory of embarrassment haunts them whenever they need to address a group of people.

CHAPTER 2

CHOOSING THE RIGHT APPROACH

Overcoming social phobia may take a great commitment, time, effort and in some cases, money. To pick the right solution, you will need the right information. Traditionally social anxiety disorders are treated using medication or/and cognitive behavioral therapy. Most clinicians use anti-depressant medications as first line of treatment of social phobia. Four major classes of drugs used in the treatment of social phobia include Selective Serotonin Reuptake Inhibitors (SSRIs) Selective Norepinephrine Reuptake Inhibitor (SNRIs), Benzodiazepines and Tricyclic Antidepressants.

Some researchers think that combining medications with psychotherapy may provide better results in case of severe anxiety disorder.

Social phobia is a treatable condition. In recent years there has been tremendous interest in the treatment of this condition.

Lots of treatment approaches have been developed and people have more treatment options available today than ever before. However finding the right doctor or therapist to treat social phobia may not be easy. Apart from CBT, other therapeutic approaches available for the treatment of social anxiety may include, Interpersonal Psychotherapy (IPT), Supportive Psychotherapy, Psychoanalysis and Analytically Oriented Psychotherapy, and Virtual Reality Therapy.

As everyone is unique, one treatment that is effective for an individual may not suit another. There is no one-size-fits-all solution for social anxiety. Sometimes picking the right treatment can be confusing.

Self-help treatment has gained popularity in recent years. The main advantage of self-help treatment is anyone can try it and it does not require direct assistance of a doctor or therapist. In self-help approach, you're taking responsibility of your own wellness.

Everyone can benefit from self-help program and it is free of cost. If you're undergoing treatment for your anxiety, you can still try self-help program. However if you are doing well enough with medication or therapy alone, adding a second therapy at the beginning would be a waste of time. In this case, you can take sequential approach. Try one approach at a time.

Start with one form of treatment and give it your best shot. Once you're done, evaluate your progress. If you find that anxiety is still there, switch to the next form of treatment.

Most treatments come with side effects. Medicines for example, they will only work as long as you take them. Quit them, the symptoms will resurface. Sometimes even psychotherapies make people uncomfortable.

The self-help program included in this book will teach the readers how to cultivate a kinder and gentler relationship with the anxious mind and body. Unlike traditional psychotherapies, this program does not encourage you to go after your fear directly. It rather focuses on mindful acceptance, self-compassion and commitment.

CONQUERING SOCIAL ANXIETY

Social anxiety is not a medical condition, although the sufferers often mistake their condition for a medical illness. It is not a disease that should be cured. Therefore overcoming social anxiety is not like recovering from a disease. It is rather like restoring the balance and harmony, and getting your life back on track. The methods you're learning in this book don't need to be beat into the ground. Take a gentle but firm approach to them.

Set aside at least thirty minutes (this can be split up if necessary) of your day practicing the methods described in this book. Make sure to maintain regularity. This book will work for you only if you work with it.

Be patient with yourself. Changes will take time. You symptoms did not come overnight, so they will not go away overnight. If you are sincere and stick your practice, you will start to notice positive changes within a couple of weeks.

Remember to give yourself credit for your efforts. As you work through the methods, give yourself a pat on the back as often as possible. Celebrate the small positive changes, rather than blaming yourself for not yet reaching your ultimate goal. Remember, your small improvement will ultimately lead to larger ones in time if you stick to your practice.

We recommend that you practice one exercise per week. It takes a while to learn a new skill and apply in your life. Therefore you have to resist the temptation to read several chapters at once, because it will make you overwhelmed.

If you're already taking prescription medications on "as needed" basis, try to avoid them, when you're doing the exercises. If you must take medications on daily basis, discuss with your doctor or therapist whether you can reduce or quit the medications.

DEALING WITH NEGATIVE THOUGHTS

Automatic negative thinking is the heart of social phobia. It takes practice and persistence to change the negative thought patterns, but your effort will be paid off by significant decrease of anxiety symptoms.

Negative thoughts, perceptions, expectations and attributions make people excessively self-conscious. Individuals with social anxiety spend lots of time focusing on their thoughts, feelings and actions. While self-consciousness is sometimes a healthy sign of emotional maturity, high level of self-consciousness stops you being natural. Heightened state of self-consciousness can leave you feeling awkward and nervous. When you're self-conscious, you can't adequately focus on the people you're interacting with. As a result, you might miss important information. Your lack of attention can make others think that you're not interested in them. That will make them lose interest in you.

Learning to shift your attention from yourself to others is an effective way to deal with negative thoughts and reduce social anxiety. You always have a choice to move your focus to some aspect of the situations you are in. For instance, when you're listening to a song, you can focus and carefully listen to the lyrics. You may need to keep reminding yourself to maintain the focus. Other aspects of the song such as the music may grab your attention for a while, but you can bring your attention back on the lyrics.

Same rule is applied when you interact with someone. You can always choose to rest your attention on the other person rather than yourself.

Focus your attention on the person you're interacting with whenever you feel self-conscious. It may need some degree of practice in the beginning, but overtime you will learn to be more attentive. Shifting the attention is a good strategy for coping with mild anxiety in any social situation. Here are the techniques you have to follow:

1. Remind yourself to pay attention to others when your self-consciousness makes you nervous.

2. Pay your complete attention to the words and ideas of your partner.

3. As you're listening, think about how the other person feels about the information they are sharing with you. Is

he/she talking about something that means a lot to them? Or is he or she just giving away some routine information?

4. Sometimes you will find your attention is switched to your own feelings and you're having anxious thoughts. Just ignore the negative thoughts and move your attention back on the conversation. The anxious thoughts get stronger when you pay attention to them.

5. You don't have to be worried about what you'll say next. If you are an attentive listener, you'll find that your own ideas that you'll say next are coming spontaneously.

6. We can never know what others exactly think about us. Therefore thinking about how others may perceive us is a waste of time. So during a conversation, don't try to figure out what the other person thinking about you. It will only make you more nervous.

The above approach can be applied only to manage mild social anxiety. When your anxiety level is high, shifting the attention won't be easy. We will take a different approach in this case.

When we allow negative thoughts occupy our mind without interruption, we unwittingly build a prison in our own mind. Eventually we become a prisoner of our thoughts. In order to break free our inner mental prison of negativity, we have to break the negative thought patterns. There are many different ways to break the patterns of negative thinking. One of the effective ways is to notify or tell the brain that you don't want those negative thoughts. Make a statement to yourself. It will be more effective if you say it out loud. It may sound a little strange, but unless you tell your mind that you don't like those anxious thoughts, the mind will continue to support the habitual pattern of negative thinking. Making the statement out loud will help your mind realize that you're having the negative thoughts more often than usual.

Whenever you find yourself having a negative thought, say, "Stop!" and visualize a bright red stop sign or stop light. Then say to yourself, "I've just stopped a negative thought from making me feel bad. These negative thoughts can bring only pain. They never help. I choose to think positive thoughts".

You can make your own statements. But make sure to keep them simple.

If you're not good at visualizing, you can make statements like, "Wait a minute! Negative thoughts are tricking me again. These thoughts drain my energy. I won't let that happen. I choose to think positive".

Both of these methods work. Use either one you want.

The statement you make to yourself has to be rational and true, something your brain can comprehend.

If making a statement every time makes you feel uncomfortable, try whispering "Stop" whenever a negative thought arises. Over time just imagine hearing "stop" inside your head. The point is to break the pattern of unhealthy thinking by interrupting the negative thought process.

To get your mind off the negative thinking track, find an engaging activity. We can call it "distraction". A good "distraction" can be reading a book, listening to music, trying a new recipe, taking care of the garden, swimming, even doing household chores can be included in the list of distraction. As everyone has different interests and likes, it is important to choose an activity that you love, an activity that can shift your mind completely off the negative thought process.

As negative thinking is a major element of social anxiety, we have to take more than one approach to break this thought pattern and develop a positive thinking habit. We will discuss more approaches in the next chapter.

CHAPTER 3

DEFINING THE COGNITIVE THINKING ERRORS

We already know that automatic negative thoughts are the irrational thoughts about oneself, the world and the future. These thoughts are irrational because when we try to think them over, we always find something about them that is illogical in some way. The logical errors in automatic negative thoughts are called cognitive thinking errors. Dr. Judith Beck in her book Cognitive therapy: Basics and Beyond (1995) outlined a number of cognitive thinking errors. Before we get into the details of different thinking errors, there are a couple of things you have to keep in mind.

1. There are different aspects of a thought. Depending on what aspect you focus, a negative thought can contain several thinking errors.

2. No matter how severe you think your anxiety symptoms are, you can overcome them. Therefore if you identify lots of thinking errors in your own thoughts, there is nothing to be worried about.

Understanding the thinking errors is important, because it will help us recognize and resolve our faulty way of thinking that generates anxiety. Now let us review each of the thinking errors in detail:

Black and white thinking: (also called polarized thinking or all or nothing thinking). This thinking error makes you obsessed with perfection. This pattern of thinking will tell you that you either do a thing perfectly or don't do at all. When you have this thinking error, you will have high expectation of yourself, which can push you to put more effort in an activity to attain perfection. But the downside is it can make you mentally paralyzed by discouraging you from trying something because you might not do it perfectly. Black and white thinking can make you believe that nothing is ever good enough, which gives way to social anxiety. Here is an example of black and white thinking:

Think about a person who has thinking error: "Women will only date me if I look handsome." In his case, looking "handsome" meant looking like a model or movie star. As black and white thinking has no shades of grey, you're either in a good category or in a bad category. Therefore, as the man does not consider himself to be "Handsome", he sees himself as "unattractive". This lowers his self-esteem and generates the fear of rejection.

This is the cognitive error that tells you that you're never perfect, that you can't socialize, that you'll say or do something embarrassing in social situations.

Overgeneralization: This negative propensity of the mind may make us view any negative situation that occurs as being an unlimited pattern of setbacks and defeat. You may take one isolated event and generalize it in all other circumstances. Here is an example:

Consider a public speaking event and a person is addressing a group of people. "Good morning ladies and gentleman. I'm really excited to be here and ..." Silence.... Nothing. His speech stopped.

Now this situation is embarrassing. If the person has overgeneralization error, he will think, "this bad thing happened, so I know that will always happen". Next time before participating in a public speaking event, he will have thoughts like, "I know I won't be able to speak before an audience because last time I got very anxious and embarrassed myself". He will predict the negative outcome based on just one previous instance. Overgeneralization means not giving yourself a second chance.

Selective abstraction: Selective abstraction or mental filter makes people dwell on the negative aspects of any situation while overlooking anything positive. They fail to see any bright side, as if they are wearing negative glasses that only let negative things and filter out the good aspects. For example, one attends a social event and afterward focuses on the one awkward look directed her way, and ignores the signal of receptiveness and positive gestures from rest of the people.

Selective abstraction has the potential to turn thoughts in self-fulfilling prophecies. By constantly focusing and rehearsing on the dark sides of something we actually reinforce that idea and unwittingly act to bring it into reality. Say for example, if you are going through a written test, and constantly thinking that you are running out of time, you may find it hard to concentrate, you may rush and make mistakes and may fail to answer all the questions within the time limit. When we are habituated in selective abstraction, things often appear different than they actually are, and hence create a distorted perception of reality.

Diminishing the positive: The mediaeval alchemists dreamt of inventing a method for transmuting base metals into gold. This cognitive thinking error can bring forth a talent for doing the exact opposite; that is turning your golden joy into emotional lead. That's why Dr. Burns calls it reverse alchemy. Diminishing the positive is: you twist positive into negative ones. You tend to reject a positive experience by insisting that it does not count for one reason or another. You may subconsciously try to explain why it was a fluke. People who tend to diminish the positive fails to explain a subject logically because they are using a double standard. They count the negative evidences no matter how irrational or irrelevant they seem, and abandon positive evidences no matter how strong and persuasive they sound.

Jumping to conclusions: The tendency of jumping to conclusion is a very common thinking error. People with this error often become quick to jump to conclusion about a person or situation. A social phobic just believes this as true without enquiring the fact first. Jumping to conclusion thoughts have two categories; one is mindreading, another is fortune telling.

Mindreading: We were not born with the ability to read someone's mind nor to see things form someone else's point-of-view. Yet we can't resist the impulse of assuming what someone is thinking. People with social anxiety often make the false assumptions that other people are looking down on them or think they are stupid or boring. Have you ever caught yourself frequently having thoughts like, "My co-workers think that I am lazy", "My manager must be mad at me" or "My subordinates think that I'm weird"? If you have, instead of absolutes, rephrase the statement as a possibility (like they might think...).

Fortune telling: Fortune telling is another "jumping to conclusion" thinking habit. When a social phobic person with this thinking error looks ahead to the future, they see only misery— there is no hope, no future... "There is nothing to look forward to; hopes are useless to have; no matter how much I try, I will end up with failure." Or they predict their future like "I will never have a normal life" or "today is going to be horrible". By repeating these kinds of statements subconsciously over and over again, people turn them into powerful beliefs, which aggravates their anxiety.

The binocular trick: With binoculars we can see distant objects closer and larger. But if we look into a pair of binoculars the wrong way, everything looks faraway and smaller. Binocular trick is a thinking error that makes us view negative things out of proportions and positive things unusually small. Being accustomed in binocular trick we subconsciously put proportionately greater emphasis on a perceived failure, weakness or threat and lesser emphasis on perceived success, strength and opportunity. Catastrophization falls under the spectrum of magnification, where people blow their anxious thoughts out of proportion until they becomes extremely distressing for them. For example, you have done a minor mistake in your workplace and fearing that you may lose your job as a result. Catastrophization occurs when we look to the future and seriously analyze all the things that may go wrong; then start to believe "it's bound to all go wrong for me."

Emotional reasoning: When we are anxious, we may allow emotional reasoning to guide us. Emotional reasoning assumes that what you feel must be true. We can overcome most of the thinking errors with rational thinking, but emotional reasoning makes it quite challenging. If we continue to take for granted the dark thoughts that give rise to negative feeling and try to reason on the basis of that feeling, we may find ourselves lost in the maze of anxiety. Emotional reasoning substitutes emotion for evidence. The basic assumption for emotional reasoning is, "if there is smoke, there must be fire". For example, "I feel guilty, therefore I must have done something wrong". If our decisions are driven by emotions, and the facts contradict the feelings, it can be very damaging for our psychological health. As smoke is not the firm evidence of fire, feeling is not the evidence of reality. We have to learn to question the feeling, and enquire if it is real.

Should and must statements: Should and must statements are common negative thinking patterns that contribute to anxiety. Negative thinkers often use the phrases that contain should or must as a way to take on a pessimistic view in their life. These statements arise as the emotional consequence of guilt. When a socially anxious person directs should or must statements towards themselves or others, they often feel irritated, guilty, resentful or frustrated. Frequent use of these statements can cause a great deal of emotional distress to the anxiety sufferer. These statements often surface automatically without the involvement of our conscious mind. Here are the examples of should and must statements, "I should never get upset with my partner" or "I feel badly about the speech I just delivered, therefore I must have been a bad speaker." Using these statements often leads to unrealistic expectations, which can augment social anxiety.

Labeling and mislabeling: Anxious minds use a negative operating system and tend to focus on the dark side. People with this thinking error frequently label themselves and others with demeaning labels. Labeling and mislabeling is overgeneralization at its worst. Every one of us makes mistakes. Then we forget or learn from mistakes and move on.

But a person with this thinking error builds a self images based on the errors they have made. As a result people may view themselves as losers. Social anxiety can also make people label others negatively. In this case they may unconsciously nurture destructive emotions like hostility, jealousy, and hatred. Most of the demeaning labels used by the negative mind is not real, they are mislabels. These labels are generated from the distorted perception of reality. 'Labeling and mislabeling' ruins self-esteem.

Personalization: Personalization makes people take things personally. People with this thinking error may feel responsible for other's anger for failure, for bad weather, or for a host of uncontrollable circumstances. For example, teenagers with social anxiety may suffer from guilt when their parents get divorced; because they believe it's their fault. People with severe personalization tendency may find themselves blaming for virtually everything. When a crisis erupts, they immediately think, "I must have done something wrong". They may even obsessively keep reviewing the incident to find a reason to blame themselves.

THE VOICE OF ANXIETY AND RATIONAL RESPONSE

Now you have some understanding on logical errors in negative thinking and you know how to break the pattern of automatic thinking using the negative thought stoppage technique. Challenging the irrational thoughts is a CBT technique, which is used for decreasing the level of social anxiety and creating a more positive outlook and lifestyle.

When you experience negative self-talks, use these questions to challenge your thoughts:

- Am I falling into the cycle of negative thinking, e.g. catastrophizing (magnification of binocular trick) or overestimating danger?

- Do I have any evidence the thought is true? If not, what evidence do I have that it is not true?

- Have I confused a thought with a fact?

- If a friend of mine had the same thought, what would be my advice to him/her?

- What would a friend say about my thought?

- Do I know for certain that _________________

  Example: Do I know for certain that they will dislike me?

- Am I 100% sure that___________

  Example: Am I 100% sure that I will embarrass myself?

- How many times has that happened before?

- What is the worst that could happen?

- Is _________________so important that my future depends on it?

  Is making everyone like me instantly is so important that my future depends on it?

- If it did happen, how could I cope with that?

- Is there any other explanation for _______________

  Example: Is there another explanation for why she ignored me?

- Does is really mean_________________

  Example: Does it really mean I'm unattractive?

If you spend some time challenging the automatic negative thoughts, you'll find that your automatic thoughts blow things out of proportion and makes you feel miserable. Identify the negative thoughts, find the thinking errors, and then challenge those thoughts.

By challenging those thoughts you'll learn that negative thoughts are the voice of anxiety. This voice becomes stronger when you believe in it. This voice of anxiety, exaggerates, catastrophizes, puts us down, makes us feel guilty, robs us of our self-esteem and makes us very pessimistic.

Spend 15 minutes everyday challenging the voice of anxiety. Don't over-practice.

Developing rational response: Learning to question your thoughts may take time and practice, but it's worth the effort. The negative self-talk can be proved irrational by questioning the thoughts, but you will also need to develop a rational response to defeat the voice of anxiety. Rational response is about taking a positive or at least a neutral view about a situation or symptoms. There are three ways to talk back to an automatic negative thought:

Rational response #1: *"This thought is not true" or "This thought is not completely true".*

Example: You are worried about an upcoming work presentation.

Negative thought, "My voice will start shaking and I will end up looking like a fool."

Rational response, "This thought is not true. I had been in a situation like this before and I did well". Or "This thought is not completely true. Even if someone notices that I'm nervous, that does not mean that they will think badly of me".

Rational response #2: *"So what!" "Who cares!" or "It's not a big deal"*.

Whenever you find your negative thoughts making you feel uncomfortable, use these rational responses.

Example: Thought- "I was very quiet at the meeting".

Rational response: "So what! My colleagues still seem to like me even though I'm sometimes very quiet. It's no big deal."

Rational response #3: *I can do something about that.*

Example: Thought- "They are going to notice me panicking. I'll make a fool of myself"

Rational response: "I will take a few deep breaths. It will make me feel relaxed. It's ok to feel a little nervous."

Don't use just one type of rational response all the time. It's a mistake many people make. For example some people habitually respond, "It's a lie. It's lie. It's lie". But what if it is true? Therefore sometimes you have to say, "Hold on. May be this is not completely true or I can do something about that." Here is an example:

You are having a distressing thought: "nobody loves me" and you habitual response is, *"So what! Who cares"*! Well that's not true. We do care if somebody loves us. Instead you can say, "My parents love me, my sister love me, my friends love me."

Sometimes thinking about the absolutely worst thing that could happen can lead to good rational responses. For example, your worst fear is, being rejected by someone, looking silly or being temporarily embarrassed. Your rational response would be, *"I can live with that."* If your worst fear is something serious, such as losing a job, missing promotion or losing your marriage, then you have to spend some time thinking about how likely that can happen. That can lead to the rational response of, "the worst that can happen is ________________, but that is unlikely.

POSITIVE SELF-TALK DURING ANXIETY ATTACKS

When we feel overwhelmed with anxiety, our mind races with negative thoughts. We desperately try to fight those intrusive voices and the emotions that come with it, which only worsens our situation. Instead of fighting those racing intrusive thoughts, we can use positive self-talks to manage those anxious moments. We can replace the voice of anxiety with rational, realistic self-talk or coping statements. Here are some of the positive statements you can use when you feel overwhelmed with anxiety:

1. I'm feeling uncomfortable right now, but I can handle it.

2. I know fighting does not help— I choose not to fight. Anxiety shrinks when I quit fighting.

3. I can still focus on the task in hand. By staying present and focused on my task, my anxiety decreases.

4. Although I'm feeling anxious, I can still relax.

5. This is not an emergency. I can take all the time I need to let go and relax.

6. Having this feeling is an opportunity for me to learn to cope with my fears. The more I learn, the stronger I become.

7. This sensation is uncomfortable, but it is not dangerous. It can't hurt me.

8. I've survived every time I went through this feeling, and I will survive this time too.

9. Anxiety is an old habit pattern that my body responds to. I'll break this old habit pattern eventually. I feel a little bit of peace despite my anxiety. This peace will grow and my anxiety will disappear. I only have to stick to my practice and wait patiently.

10. Anxious thoughts and feelings can only make me feel down if I pay attention to them. But I refuse to focus on these things. Instead, I will talk slowly to myself, and continue with the task in my hand. If the anxiety does not get my attention, it will shrink.

CHAPTER 4

GIVING UP THE STRUGGLE

Logic tells us that in a threatening situation we have to either fight the threat, or run for safety. If our body perceives a situation as threatening, it initiates the emergency responses— tenses the muscles, heightens the blood pressure and accelerates the heartbeat. If our mind perceives an emotion as threatening, it also either fights to defeat it or tries to escape it. Here are some of the negative mindsets we use while dealing with social anxiety.

- We insist that we should not feel this way— "Why should I be scared of the world outside? Why being a center of attention makes me so nervous? Why a social event or group activity makes me feel awkward and uncomfortable? I shouldn't.

- We use anger to fight the anxious feeling— "Enough is enough! I'm sick and tired living a life like this. I want a normal life. I want peace. I hate feeling like a loser or coward".

- We bemoan the fact that we have anxiety— "Why me? Everyone I know has a good social life. They can do whatever they want. My social life is almost non-existent. How come I developed this problem? No one else I know has this! I don't see any hope. I have to spend rest of my life with social anxiety."

- We use the fairness argument— "This is so unfair! Why do I have to have this problem? I did not do anything wrong! It is just not fair that I'm the only person who has to deal with this terrible problem!"

- We use deserving argument— "I don't deserve this suffering! I'm a good person. I've been nice to everyone. I've never harmed anyone. What have I done to deserve this?

Now, this is quite normal to use these inner-talks to react to the painful feeling that social phobia generates. Here our mind is desperately seeking all the options to get rid of this terrible emotional pain.

But unfortunately using those negative self-talks to escape anxiety is like struggling in a quicksand. Fight and flail around and you sink. Lie flat, keep still, start making slow gentle movement and you'll be able to roll out of it. The way to get yourself free is counterintuitive.

If you fight anxiety or get angry will anxiety, you are unknowingly making anxiety stronger. Think anxiety as a "pseudo-emotion", and learn not to follow what anxiety is telling you. Your anxiety wants you to fight, to get aggressive, and to beat yourself up, because doing it will make it stronger. Our "common-sense" ways of coping with anxiety will never work. You will be dragged further down into the pit. Instead, do the opposite of what you are initially tempted to do. That's why the solution to "social anxiety" is called a "paradox".

Social anxiety is a great bluffer. Don't trust this emotion— it tells you that you're in danger when you are perfectly safe. Don't try to resist your anxiety— what you resist persists.

Do NOT fight your anxiety, because the energy you use fighting this emotion adds to its intensity. The best way to cope with anxiety is the simplest— that is "TO DO NOTHING".

If you don't fight, your anxiety will disappear. Therefore don't react or respond. Slow down, you can use some rational statements. Say to yourself, "Anxiety wants mc to fight, because it feeds on my fear and anger. If I fight anxiety, it grows. If I do nothing, it withers. I choose not to fight anxiety" Anxiety is like a ghost, an invisible opponent— you can't defeat it by fighting.

ANXIETY QUICK FIX

This is not a "cure" for social anxiety. But it's an effective temporary fix: Whenever you feel overwhelmed with anxiety, check your breathing. When we feel tensed, our breath becomes short and shallow. When we feel relaxed our breath becomes slow and deep. Therefore how we feel changes the way we breathe. The opposite is also true— how we breathe can change the way we feel. Try the following method when your anxiety level is high.

Place your right hand below your belly button and left hand a couple of inches below your collar bone.

Take a deep breath through your nose while counting slowly from one to five in your mind. Take the air inside your belly. Allow your abdomen to stretch as you breath-in.

Now hold your breath and mentally count from one to five.

As you exhale slowly, allow your abdomen to contract. Breathe out to the count of eight. Remember, exhalation should be longer than inhalation.

Now hold again to the count of five. Then begin again.

This is a temporary solution, but it really works. If you aren't used to conscious breathing, you'll be amazed to discover how controlled breathing changes our state of mind.

Getting active also temporarily cut down the feeling of anxiety. Because during anxiety our system releases a hormone called adrenaline. Adrenaline speeds up our thinking process, and we experience a storm of negative thoughts. The best way to reduce the level of adrenaline is to burn it off by being physically active. Another hormone released during anxiety is cortisol, which is responsible for generating the feeling of fear. If you engage in a physical activity and keep the focus on external things, both adrenaline and cortisol level will drop.

EXPOSURE METHODS

Exposure is major component of virtually every cognitive behavioral treatment protocol for anxiety disorders. The purpose of exposure is to teach the social phobic individuals how to face the feared situations so that they can discover first hand whether or not their feared expectations are likely to occur and how well they can cope. Exposure is normally conducted with the assistance of a therapist as a part of CBT program. The clients are encouraged to repeatedly face the feared situations to find out that they can socialize, that people don't care if they display anxiety symptoms (blushing, sweating, shaking etc.), that people enjoy their company and so forth. Clients may experience some anxiety during this process, but short-term pain will lead to long-term gain. Exposure is performed using various systematic techniques, and these techniques are specifically tailored considering the nature and severity of anxiety. However exposure is not one-size-fits-all solution for social anxiety. In this book, we won't recommend you to force yourself to face your most feared situations; because exposure should be gradual and should be performed in the safe environment. Facing your fear without preparation can sometime worsen your condition. We will learn two different types of exposures in this chapter. We will learn to face your fears without facing our fears for real.

INTEROCEPTIVE EXPOSURE

Interoceptive exposure is used specifically to overcome the fear of physical symptoms of social anxiety. You don't have to face a feared situation or object; you will rather be exposed to a particular physical sensation like racing heart, shaking or sweating. By being repeatedly exposed to the physical sensations, you'll learn that these anxiety symptoms are harmless.

These exposure techniques are designed to be uncomfortable but not painful. One should be generally in good health before attempting these techniques. If you have conditions like heart disease, epilepsy or seizures, asthma or lung problems and neck and back conditions, it is advised to consult your physician before trying these exercises. Here some interoceptive exposure techniques:

Exercise: Shake your head from side to side for thirty seconds.

This exposure will replicate anxiety symptoms including dizziness/feeling faint, pounding/racing heart and breathlessness.

Exercise: Place your head between your knees for thirty seconds then lift your head quickly to normal position.

Symptoms most strongly elicited with this exercise include dizziness or feeling faint, pounding/racing heart and breathlessness.

Exercise: Spin around while standing at a medium pace for one minute.

Strongly elicited symptoms are dizziness or feeling faint, breathlessness and pounding/racing heart.

Exercise: Breathe through a narrow straw for two minutes. Breathe in an out with your mouth. Make sure not to breathe through the nose.

This exercise will mimic the anxiety symptoms including breathlessness, choking and pounding/racing heart.

Exercise: Stare at a mirror for a minute or two.

Most elicited symptoms are feeling unreal or in a dream and dizziness.

Exercise: Sit facing a heater for five minutes.

This exercise will replicate the anxiety symptoms including hot flushes/chills, sweating and breathlessness.

Exercise: Use a tongue depressor.

Elicited symptoms are choking, nausea/abdominal distress and breathlessness/smothering sensations.

Do these exercises only if you are too much worried about the physical symptoms of panic attacks.

IMAGINAL EXPOSURE

Social anxiety makes us to avoid different people, places, objects and situations. It also makes us avoid our own fearful thoughts. We develop so much fear about our own anxious thoughts that we try to suppress them. We go to great lengths to not to picture the disastrous consequences that we fear could occur if we speak in front of a group of people or face the situations we avoid at any cost. This thought suppression actually leads to an increase in the frequency of thoughts we try not to have. While pushing thoughts away might feel very practical, it unfortunately does not work.

Think anything else but pink elephants. You will find that it will be all you can think of. Therapists specialized in treating social anxiety often use the "pink elephant" examples to help their patients understand the concept of thought suppression. Any thought you try to suppress will come back with greater frequency and intensity. If you allow yourself to have the thoughts by purposefully bringing them on, you will find that these thoughts are not dangerous. If you practice not to suppress your thoughts, you will experience a decrease in the frequency of your fears and worries. Imaginal exposure is aimed to reduce your fear of thoughts of images and prepare you to face your fears with confidence.

Sit comfortably and close your eyes. Breathe in and out deeply and slowly. Now vividly imagine yourself in a social situation you fear most. For example, imagine yourself giving a speech in front of a small audience. Make it an event of glory in your mind. Imagine vividly— look at the audience, make eye contact. Imagine that you're speaking spontaneously, eloquently. Visualize yourself as an active participant, rather than a passive observer. Notice all the sights, smells, sensations and sound around you. Spend five minutes visualizing yourself being a center of attention. Imagine people are eager to listen what you have to say. Imagine that people are getting inspired by your words.

Don't try hard. If you can't bring the image, don't worry. Bring the feeling; the image will follow. Don't over-practice. Do this exercise once a day for ten minutes.

CHAPTER 5

THE ART OF ACCEPTANCE

"People have a hard time letting go of their suffering. Out of a fear of the unknown, they prefer suffering that is familiar." ~Thich Nhat Hanh"

We have already learned that struggling your anxious feelings makes your anxiety stronger. We already know 'what we resist, persists'. If we quit fighting the anxious feelings, stop reacting to anxious thoughts and emotions, the anxiety loses its grip and starts to shrink. But what if we accept anxiety? By accepting anxiety what I mean is, we will not just stop fighting the anxiety but embrace the experience of anxious thoughts, memories, sensations and feelings as they are, without judging them. The solution to anxiety is paradoxical. If you quit fighting anxiety, it will shrink; if you accept anxiety, it will disappear.

But acceptance is a process that does not come easily or naturally for most of us. We tend to see the world through the glasses of our own judgments and preconceived notions of what is and what should be. This is especially true for the people with social anxiety who are overwhelmed with self-doubt and what-if thoughts. In order to change perception about the world, we have to allow ourselves to experience the world directly, unedited— the way it is. Acceptance has a transformative power, which will only work if you learn to accept anxiety the way it is, through firsthand experience. Acceptance is not about liking your anxious feelings, nor it is about approving what happened or did not happened to you. It is not about seeing things from a different viewpoint. It is about taking an open, honest and courageous move to acknowledge and experience things as they are. It's about being compassionate to ourselves and being proactive.

Acceptance is not about giving up. By embracing acceptance, we are actually making room for improvement; we are regaining the energy and time that might otherwise be wasted on changing something that can't or needn't be changed.

Some of us may find it difficult in the beginning to confront the anxiety-related thoughts, images and feelings willingly and move on. But this is what we should do to get on the path of living. Remember, acceptance is way easier than rejection. But we've allowed ourselves to get so accustomed to non-acceptance or rejection overtime, that now we find struggling easier than non-struggling. When you accept, you don't have to fight the battle or tug of war with your thoughts and feelings.

INTRODUCING MINDFULNESS

Mindfulness is a psychological process that focuses on acceptance, acknowledgement and compassion. The word mindfulness was derived from the Pali term *sati*. Thomas William Rhys Davids a scholar of Pali first used this term in 1881 when he translated Buddhist scripture Sati. But the person who popularized this meditation in the west is Jon Kabrat-Zinn, the professor of Medicine Emeritus at the University of Massachusetts Medical School. Since the beginning of mindfulness movement in 1970's this ancient meditation has been increasingly gaining popularity for its potentials for treating various physical, psychological and psychosomatic ailments. Those who practice mindfulness and integrate the teachings of this philosophy in their lives, live a life of fullness and joy. Although mindfulness was originated from an ancient Buddhist meditation, the pioneers of mindfulness stripped off its religious aspects to make it simple for non-Buddhists and the general.

ASPECTS OF MINDFULNESS

According to Kabat-Zinn (1990), mindfulness is about making direct contact with our present experience, with acceptance and without judgment. Imagine observing your internal or external experience taking a neutral but nurturing perspective— this is what mindfulness is like. The process of mindfulness has three components: paying attention on purpose, paying attention in the present moment and paying attention nonjudgmentally, with acceptance. Let us discuss each of the components.

Paying attention in the present moment: In mindfulness, your consciousness should be anchored in the present moment in the unfolding of your direct experience from moment to moment (your direct experience is what is registered by five senses: sight, hearing, smell, touch and taste).

Paying attention nonjudgmentally with acceptance: When we pay mindful attention to something, we experience it without judgment, without imposing any qualities. This way we accept something the way it is, without attempting to change it or escape it.

MINFULNESS AND ANXIETY MANAGEMENT

It is important to know that mindfulness must not be used as a strategy to manage or control your anxiety, although most people unwittingly try to use mindfulness to control their anxious feelings. For instance mindful breathing is relaxing, but it is not designed as a relaxation technique. Beginners of mindfulness may attempt mindful breathing to get immediate relief from anxiety. But it is not recommended. Mindfulness is rather a defusion strategy aimed for aiding people to confront their experiences as they are, without all the other evaluative baggage including attribution, verbal rules and reasons that usually accompany it. Purpose of mindfulness is not making you feel calm and relaxed, although calmness and relaxation comes as a byproduct of mindfulness. During the process of mindfulness, you may also experience distressing thoughts, emotions and memories. Whatever you experience is, you're supposed to experience it fully without avoidance and escaping.

Purpose of using acceptance and mindfulness as a method for overcoming anxiety, is to help you wake up in your own experiences as a fully functional human being. Your self-realization will liberate you from the delusion of social anxiety. We must not use mindfulness as a new way of avoiding or fixing our anxious feelings. This will reinforce the old control pattern, which will prevent lasting changes.

EXERCISE # ACCEPTANCE OF THOUGHTS AND EMOTIONS

Observing the breath is a core contemplative practice of traditional Buddhist meditation and a major element modern mindfulness meditation. In this exercise we will rest our focus on the breath, because our thoughts, feelings and bodily sensations are constantly changing, just like our breathing. The goal is to maintain attention on the process of breathing and allowing other internal events (such as thoughts and feeling) come and go in our minds.

To practice this mindfulness meditation exercise, sit in a comfortable position. You can sit on a chair, on your bed, on a couch, or on the floor. If you are sitting on a chair, make sure that your feet are touching the ground with legs uncrossed. Sit comfortably with your back straight and chin up. Place your hands on your lap one on top of another with palms facing up.

If you have back pain, or you feel difficulty in sitting upright for few minutes, you can practice this exercise in a reclining posture at about a forty-five degree angle. In this case, you can use a foam wedge, or pillows to support your torso. You can practice this meditation also in reclining position if you are feeling ill. Keep your eyes and mouth closed during the practice.

Remember the aim of this exercise is not to make your feel different, better or relaxed; this may happen or it may not. The goal is to be present with your breath, with your thoughts, feelings and sensations.

Once you close your eyes, allow your mind to settle (10 seconds). Now take some time to get in touch with the inflow and outflow of your breath (10 seconds). Now shift your awareness to the physical sensations. Feel the contact of your body with the chair or floor. Feel the pressure or the warmth. Feel the firmness or softness of the seat. If you experience any twitching or tingling sensation anywhere in the body, move your awareness to those points. Stay with those sensations for few seconds. Bring your awareness back on your breath.

The breathing should be spontaneous. There is no need to control your breath— simply allow your breath breathe itself. Focus as you breath-in and breath-out. Be aware of the cool feeling in your nostril as you inhale and the warmth as you exhale.

Notice your stomach expands with every inhalation and contracts with every exhalation. Focus in an effortless way. Just stay with your breath, be present with the inflow and the outflow. Don't try hard, don't even focus actively... be a passive observer. Be one with your breathing. Boredom may creep in... you may feel tired after a while. But that won't happen when you are being mindful. Being mindful with your breathing does not mean that you have to put rigorous focus. You only have to stay with your breath in a blissful way.

Thoughts will inevitably arise. Your mind will wander away from the process of breathing to other concerns, thoughts, worries, images, feelings and sensations. If you find yourself drifted away by thoughts, feelings or sensations, gently drift your attention back on your breath.

Make sure that you are breathing in a natural pace, don't let the process of paying attention affect the natural rhythm. Don't turn your attention into an activity; don't struggle to stay with your breath.

We are not here to fix anything or achieve anything. Therefore let go the urge to attain any particular state of mind. Let go the urge to make an effort to feel more relaxed and comfortable.

If you find your attention frequently wandering away, you can bring a quality of kindness and compassion to your awareness. Thoughts will come. Thoughts are allowed to naturally come and go. We won't in any way prevent the thoughts from appearing, nor push the thoughts out of our mind or wish the thoughts wouldn't come.... Thoughts will appear as long as we need them. The more we ask why the thoughts are there, the more they will be there.

Remember, thoughts are part of the process. Every time we are allowing a thought to blissfully come and go, we are releasing a bubble of stress from the bottom of our mind.

You can name your thoughts and feelings. This will help you to learn the difference between yourself and your thoughts and feelings. Name your thoughts and feelings as they appear in your consciousness. For instance, if you notice that you are experiencing fear, silently tell yourself, "Fear.... there is fear". Don't judge the feeling. Don't label it as good or bad. Don't impose any attribute. If you find yourself judging your feeling, just notice and silently tell yourself, "Judging...there is judging". Whatever the feeling is just name them whenever they arise in your consciousness. You can also name the thoughts as planning, resenting, blaming, longing or whatever you experience.

If you experience agitation or confusion or boredom or anything, know that it is the part of the process. Maintain your attention on your breath. Stay compassionate and non-judging when your inner-dialogues get louder. This is also a part of the process. Stay innocent. Don't bring any intention. Don't force your practice. Let it innocently unfold.

There are forces of the mind that often try to deviate you from your course. Stay neutral. However if you start to feel that a particular thought is overpowering and makes it impossible to continue, don't try to maintain your attention by force against the intrusive thought. Just allow the mind to remain easy, without trying to focus on the breath. Return to your breath when the thought is dissolved.

Notice that the bodily sensations changes from moment to moment. It may grow stronger or weaker or remain unchanged for a while. The nature of sensation may also change. But that does not matter. Breathe naturally, compassionately in to and out from your sensations and discomfort. Our aim is not feeling better, but get better with feeling.

Physical sensations can sometimes get stronger. If you find that you are unable to focus on your breath because of strong sensation or discomfort, escort your attention to the place of discomfort. Stay neutrally with this feeling, no matter how bad it seems. Be present with this feeling, until this sensation or discomfort have significantly shrunk or faded away. Normally it takes 2/3 minutes for the sensations to diminish. But if you see no sign of improvement in three minutes, continue with it in an innocent and easy way. You may lie down and relax for 5 to 10 minutes. If you fall asleep, don't mind the time, and come out when you naturally wake up. This is a sign that some big block of stress just dissolved.

At the advanced stage of meditation, your breath will slow down...your blood pressure and body temperature will drop and muscles relax — you will feel as if you are awake in deep sleep. You will feel completely enveloped in an indescribable, soft gentleness. In this level of meditation, you become the consciousness itself. There is nothing as an object for you but only your subjectivity. This state is a gift of mindfulness practice, one that comes on its own through effortless innocent practice.

Some beginners complain about shaking/tremors/convulsion-like responses while practicing mindfulness. These kinds of responses are not unusual. There can be various explanations for these symptoms. One explanation is that the process of meditation breaks up some of your established thought patterns. Your thoughts are expressed though the body by a set of muscular tensions. Your responses to stimuli are programmed into your fascia. The process of meditation can activate some of the fascia patterns in preparation for them to be restructured. Shaking, convulsions are also the expressions of the release of stress. Don't resist the movements, allow them to come and go. But don't involve in the movements in order to continue them. Don't hold this idea that, "the more I move, the more stress will be released, therefore let the movement continue." Your slightest support to promote the movements can prolong it beyond natural needs.

If the movement intensifies, and seems to be going out of control, instead of resisting it, just open your eyes. Resume your practice when the body becomes still.

When you are ready to end your practice, gradually widen your attention. Be aware of your surroundings— the sound around you. Gently open your eyes with the intention to bring this awareness to the present moment.

Practice mindfulness for twenty minutes every day. For some people sitting still for 20 minutes can be hard in the beginning. Body aches are not uncommon in the early days of meditation. This initial soreness may arise until you have more practice. If sitting for twenty minutes causes body aches, give yourself a little break after ten minutes of comfortable meditation. Then start again.

It is important to remember that misusing this practice, as a mean to control or reduce anxiety will delay your progress. It is also important to practice it regularly at least once a day at home.

EXERCISE # MINDFUL WALKING

Anxiety affects our balance. According to a new <u>research</u>, our postural sway or the amount of our balance shifts while standing upright reduces when we feel anxious. Individuals with severe social anxiety becomes so worried about how they walk that they may sometimes lose balance and stumble when passing a group of people. Walk disturbance is very common in social anxiety.

Leg weakness or jelly leg is also a common symptom of social anxiety. If you have this anxiety symptom, your legs will feel so weak that you'll think that you might not be able to walk or stand. You may also feel that your legs or knees are too stiff that they won't move as you would like them to. If you fear of losing balance or have walk disturbance symptoms, the following exercise is for you. If you don't experience these types of symptoms, this exercise is still for you. Because mindful walking connects you deeply with your body, it slows you down and helps you to restore balance. While social anxiety makes you immobile, mindful walking counteracts this tendency and channels your anxiety and nervous energy into physical activity.

It is recommended to practice this exercise in a quiet environment. You can consider doing it in your backyard. Choose the place with the least visual distraction. Avoid crowded places or the heavy traffic. You will be needed to feel secure.

Before you start this exercise, take a few deep breaths to steady the mind. Stand in a relaxed posture with your feet evenly carrying the weight of your body.

Now start your walk. As you walk mindfully, you will notice a series of nine actions:

1. In the first stage, you are in the standing position relaxing the body and paying attention on the breath.

2. As you start your walk, you lift the heel of one foot (let's say the left foot).

3. Now the toes of the left foot are in contact with the ground. You become aware of the contact and of the

feeling that arises from the contact of the earth. You also notice that when the contact changes, the feeling also changes.

4. In this stage you lift the left foot off the ground.

5. The left foot is moving forward and you realize that feeling of standing faded away as soon as you lifted the foot off the ground. Likewise the feeling of lifting the foot is no longer there as you place the left heel on the ground. When the left foot is off the ground, you balance our body on the right foot. As you move the foot, you experience subtle thoughts like — "this is the foot; this is the movement; this is the forward motion; this is the change". These thoughts appear, stay briefly then pass away. During the movements, at every stage of walking, you experience a new feeling.

6. Now the forward motion of the left foot stops.

7. The left foot is lowered

8. The left foot is placed on the ground.

9. And in the final stage you press the left foot against the ground.

10. Same cycle of movements, feeling and thoughts occur as you move the right foot.

Breathe normally, feel the movements of your leg-joints as you walk slowly and mindfully. Feel as your calf muscles and hamstrings stretch and contract with every movement. Feel the rhythm from head to toe.

Feel the gravity and stay in the present moment. Feel relaxed as you walk, accept the feeling as it is. Feel the temperature, the breeze and stay with your walk. Be with the rhythm and continue walking. Walking meditation is not a substitute of mindfulness meditation exercise. Practice this exercise for ten minutes every day.

OVERCOMING THE FEAR OF DYING

Have you noticed all your fears whether it's a fear of public speaking or introducing yourself to a room of strangers, or fear of being humiliated can be traced back to one, truly specific fear, "the fear of death"? Every fear is a fear of death in disguise. Your fears may have their own diagnoses, may be dealt differently, but at the end of the day, it's all the same fear. Here is a visualization exercise for overcoming the fear of death.

Get yourself comfortable. Sit or lie down. Close your eyes. Take a few deep breaths. Now imagine that you are observing your own funeral. Imagine yourself in an open casket. Feel the temperature. Smell the fresh flowers. Observe your surroundings. Hear the soft music in the background.

Now let go of your body. Let it be there as an object that is no longer yours. Imagine being completely alone.... go to the limit of your feeling.

Now take a good look around the room. What do you see?

Perhaps you can see your family, your loved ones, relatives, friends, colleagues and neighbors. Listen what they are saying about you. What is your partner saying...your parents... your kids...someone you've met one time or another...listen closely to each of them. What you hear reflects how you want the people that you care about you to remember.

Now keep imagining the situation, while remembering the comments in your head. Perhaps one of them said, "He always looked nervous. I wish he'd done more with his life." Or "He was a very quiet gentle soul."

Stay with this image for a while. Now gently come back to your living body. Your life is not over yet. You still have time to be the person you want. Bring the feeling of love and respect for your living body. Allow this feeling to spread inside you, throughout your entire organism...then allow it spread out around you and everything. Imagine the feeling of love is circulating within you with the force of life itself. Accept this feeling... embrace this feeling... let it be in your blood, in the air you breathe.

Say to yourself, "I love and accept my body and I'm grateful to my body for holding me up and strengthening me on my path through this life. My body deserves love. I'm perfect, whole and complete just the way I am. No one can make me feel bad about myself without my permission. My existence makes the world a better place. Everyday in every way I'm getting better and better."

Now it is time to wake up. Breathe in and out for few times. Open your eyes. This exercise may seem a bit strange and somewhat worrying in the beginning. But if you stick to it, it will not just help you to overcome the fear of death but help you to overcome negative body image and improve your self-esteem.

BRINGING COMPASSION TO YOURSELF AND OTHERS

In the process of struggling with social anxiety, we beat ourselves up. We constantly criticize ourselves. We berate ourselves. We abandon ourselves. As a result we get disconnected from our true self and get trapped in the vicious cycle of anxiety. We no longer receive any soothing support, we feel alone. We see no hope.

In order to break free from the invisible vicious cycle of anxiety, we need acceptance and self-compassion. We have learned to cultivate acceptance and compassion through mindfulness meditation, but the following ancient meditation practice called loving-kindness addresses compassion more explicitly. In the following exercise we turn toward our anxiety with interest and care.

EXERCISE # LOVING KINDNESS

Find a quiet and comfortable place to practice this meditation. Sit or lie down and close your eyes. Breathe naturally and take a few moments to get in touch with physical sensations. Pay compassionate attention to the sensations of your body. Be aware of the gentle rising and falling of your chest and belly with every in-breath and out-breath. Allow yourself to breathe normally, there is no need to control your breathing.

Now imagine a picture of yourself in your mind, and say quietly to yourself, "May I be safe. May I be free from suffering. May I be at peace."

Next, think about some very close to you, the one who means a lot to you. He or she could be your spouse, your child, a family member, perhaps even a beloved pet. Bring his/her image in your mind, and say quietly, "May he/she be safe. May he/she free from suffering. May he/she be in peace."

Next, bring an image of someone you know is very ill or going through hard times. And repeat to yourself, "May he/she be safe. May he/she be free from suffering. May he/she be at peace."

Next, bring an image of someone you don't know very well. He or she could be living your neighborhood or someone you know from work. Expand your loving kindness to that person and repeat to yourself, "May he/she be safe. May he/she be free from suffering. May he/she be at peace."

Next, think about someone you don't like— someone who hurt you or wronged you in some way. This could be your boss, a colleague or celebrity whom you dislike for some reasons.

Bring their image and say to yourself, ""May he/she be safe. May he/she be free from suffering. May he/she be at peace."

Finally bring all the above people under the umbrella of loving kindness— yourself, the one close to you, one who is ill or struggling, one whom you don't know well and the one whom you dislike and repeat to yourself, ""May they be safe. May they be free from suffering. May they be at peace."

Now let go the thoughts of loving kindness and bring your attention back on your breath.

DEALING WITH SETBACKS

You are recovering from your social anxiety and finding the balance, rhythm and harmony in your life. Naturally you think you've defeated social anxiety and it left you forever. Then out of the clear blue sky and without warning— "BOOM". Those horrible symptoms flood back pretty strongly and you feel overwhelmed, defeated, hopeless and questioning your progress.

On your road to recovery from social phobia, you'll experience setbacks. This is an important part of the recovery process. Having setbacks means you are making some real progress. You've heard the phrase, old habits die hard. Your brain used the old neural pathway for many years. Therefore it is normal that your thoughts and beliefs that traveled along those pathways became ingrained, became automatic. But when you started this program, you developed new neural pathways. You've learned new concepts and methods. You've strengthened your new pathways with practice. Although your old neural pathway is shrinking, it is still there. As the brain has used the old pathway for a long time, some old association or remembrance can trigger the old habit, and you can experience a setback. However more you use the new pathway, the weaker the old one will become. And eventually a time will come when the old pathway will be completely gone. Therefore when you experience a setback, don't let that experience get you down.

The following exercise with help you to deal with setback. This method is called Emotional freedom technique (EFT) or tapping. We can also call it the virtual acupuncture method for relieving anxiety.

EXERCISE # FREEING YOUR EMOTIONS

EFT rules are simple; the sequences are straightforward, don't take long to learn. A few minutes should be enough to grasp the idea, and learn the sequences. It takes only a minute or less to complete a round.

- Use your fingertips for tapping, not your finger pads. However, if you have long nails, you can use finger pads.

- Traditionally the practitioners use two fingers together for tapping, the index and middle finger; and only one hand. But you can use all your fingers and both of your hands to cover all the points located on either sides of the body. Besides, using all fingers you can cover more areas, therefore you have less chance of missing the right acupressure point. However, many practitioners prefer traditional one-handed two-finger approach and find it work better for them. Therefore choose the approach that suits you better.

- Use some pressure while tapping, but never so hard to hurt yourself.

- While using both hands for tapping, avoid tapping simultaneously, do the alternating tapping keeping a slight time gap.

- Tapping points are not hard to remember. Make sure you memorize the points and sequences before you try; it will be lot easier.

- The ideal number for tapping is within the duration of a single breath; that's between 5 and 7 times.

- Make sure you are not wearing glasses, armbands or watches. Electronic devices may electromagnetically interfere with the process; therefore keep electronic devices away while practicing.

- You can practice EFT in public. In this case state the affirmations softly under your breath.

Locating tapping points: Here are the acupressure points used in emotional freedom technique for anxiety.

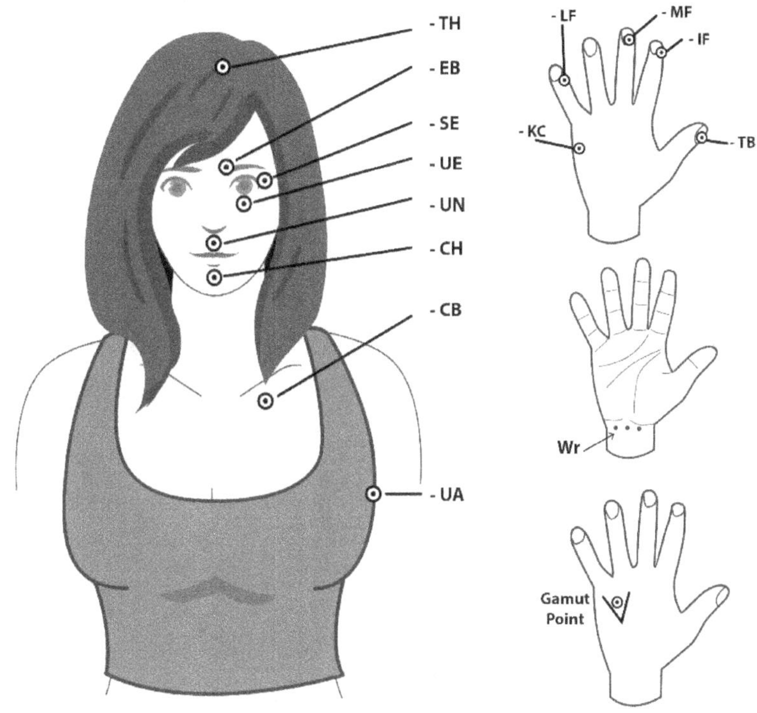

TH (Top of the head): This point is located on the tip of the head or in the center of the skull.

EB (Eyebrow): The area between the top of the nasal bone and eye socket, at the beginning of the eyebrow.

SE (Side of the eye): On the bone bordering the outside corner of the eye.

UE (Under the eye): Below the eye socket; around one inch below the pupil.

UN (Under the nose): The space between the nose and the top of the upper lip.

CH (Chin): The inward curve below the lower lip and above the chin.

CB (Collar Bone): Located on the end of the collarbone; also between the two points right at the sternum. To correctly cover this area, first place your forefinger at the bottom of the U-shaped notch at the top of the breastbone. Then slide the finger about one inch down towards the chest then move one inch left (or right).

UA (Under the Arm): The area below the armpit aligning with the nipple of men and the middle of the bra strap of women.

Wr (Wrists): Located inside the wrists.

KC (Karate chop point): This point is located at the center of the fleshy part of the outside of either hand between the wrist and the base of the little finger.

Gamut point: It is on the back of either hand and is 1/2 inch behind the midpoint between the knuckles at the base of the ring finger and the little finger.

Fingers (Tb, IF, MF, LF): Points on the inside of the curve at the bottom of each fingernails (either hand); Thumb, Index finger, Middle finger and Little finger; NOT ring finger.

We have learned the tapping points. Now let us start our journey towards emotional freedom, the freedom from all the negativities that brings anxiety and create havoc in our lives. Here are the steps.

1. Sit down gently with your spine erect and chin up. Breathe softly and slowly, allow your mind to become calm. Now raise your arms above your head and use the fingertips of both hands to tap the top your head. Tap for five times. While you are tapping, say to yourself, "Even though I feel some anxiety, I completely love, forgive and accept myself."

2. Next, the eyebrow points; tap on the right EB with your right hand fingers, then left EB with the left hand fingers for five times. Say, "Even though I feel some anxiety, I completely love, forgive and accept myself."

3. Side of the eye point on either side: Tap five times and say, "even though I feel some anxiety, I completely love, forgive and accept myself."

4. Under the eye (Both sides): Tap...Tap...Tap...Tap...Tap...and say, "Even though I feel some anxiety, I completely love, forgive and accept myself".

5. Under the nose: Tap five times, switch sides, and say, "Even though....................I completely love, forgive and accept myself"

6. Above the chin: Tap and say to yourself, "Even though.........I completely love, forgive and accept myself."

7. Collar bone: Twin points...Tap five times on each point and say, "I am such a happy person".

8. Under the arm: Use the four fingers of the right hand to tap on the left side and the four fingers of the left hand to tap on the right side. Tap five times and say, "I am soooo happy"

9. On the Karate chop point: Tap on the right hand and say "I am such a happy person". Tap on the left hand and say, "I am soooo happy."

10. On the wrist: Right wrist tap and say, "I am such a happy person". Tap on the left wrist and say, "I am soooo happy."

11. The Gamut point: While tapping on the gamut point, perform the nine actions. Tap with the eyes closed... tap with eyes open. Now, keeping the head steady, tap and look hard down right...tap and look hard down left. Tap and roll the eyes counterclockwise. Tap and roll the eyes clockwise. Now tap and hum a song (happy birthday) for five seconds...count from one to five and again hum the five seconds of the song.

12. Below the fingernails: Tap five times on each finger (except the ring finger) with the index finger of one hand, and say "I am so happy". Switch hands and follow the same instruction.

This is one round. Do another round. Make a little change in the statement when you are repeating the process. Instead of saying "Even though I feel" say "Even though I still feel".

EFT is a very flexible method. You can tap on the left or right side of your body; there is no way you can get it wrong. Assess your feeling when you are done. Are you feeling better now?

Make sure you are being completely aware of your emotions as you practice EFT. Maintain your focus on your area of tapping. Don't rush. Some degree of self-acceptance is required for getting the most out of EFT. Practice with a feeling of self-love and acceptance.

CLOSING COMMENTS

We have come to the end of our journey together. We have learned many methods. Now you are more equipped than ever to handle your anxiety. Be patient and stick to your practice. Be kind and compassionate to yourself and allow yourself to take all the time you need to overcome your anxiety. Never lose hope. Never give up. Social anxiety is a delusion, which will disappear the moment you'll realize its true nature.

www.ingramcontent.com/pod-product-compliance
Lightning Source LLC
Chambersburg PA
CBHW051906250726
48659CB00002B/508